In The Dark of the Sun
And Other Poems

by

D. Lothar Pietz

ANDU WAKUC
New House Press

Garden City, Idaho
2021

Copyright © 2021 by Andu Wakuc and D. Lothar Pietz
All rights reserved
Printed in the United States of America

ISBN 978-0-578-80737-9

Typeface used for main text is Doves Type used under license

"*In The Dark of the Sun and Other Poems* by Lothar Pietz presents a series of pieces praising life in all its challenging and redeeming phases. Lyric poems invite the reader to sit back and enjoy the style — lines written from the heart and spiced with a wry wit. Companion poems *Whispers* and *A Knowing Silence* quietly open the volume. As the ensuing selections reveal, reading Lothar's poetry is like opening the doors of a cabinet of curiosities. Poems explore a range of past and present experiences. A recent cruise on the Baltic Sea sparks a memory of Hans Brinker's heroic boyhood. A few poems illustrate how the natives of Papua New Guinea lent excitement to Lothar's youth. Psalms, days, an hourglass and a full serving of the natural world fill the discerning and humorous poetry of *In The Dark of the Sun*. A section of Notes on the Poems and a brief biography round out the volume. In closing, Lothar writes, "still at my age I have to be grateful that the moon should let me see its glory this one chance more.""

—Margaret Koger

"Lothar has a gift for writing that invites readers along for the poetic ride, as in *I Like A God* — a bold title from a man who served more than fifty years as a pastor. His poetry, however, doesn't preach. Instead, Lothar's voice welcomes you on a mental tour wherever he takes the subject. You'll gaze over the railing of the mind's back porch, explore the ambiguity of spring, and lean in when angels whisper in Lothar's ear. Along the way, you'll be treated to glimpses of humor and to insights into the condition of being human. This collection is a journey into a life lived thoughtfully, with as much certainty as searching questions, always with curiosity and wonder."

—James Armstrong

"Our monsters, the better angels of our nature, God, and culture — it's all up for discussion in Lothar's poetry collection. Sometimes there is the sense he's sharing precious and private evolving thoughts that a Lutheran Pastor might not ordinarily share. Sometimes perhaps the thoughts are conversations he's had on certain topics, time for example, which he's had with himself over decades. Over all, they convey a mood of confiding that feels privileged and communal. One's heart is stirred. And it's extraordinary!"

—Sharla Ng

"Lothar's poetry is a compilation of his keen observation of the natural world combined with his life as Pastor and scholar. He reflects on the foibles of man, sometimes tongue-in-cheek, sometimes in all seriousness. Fresh and often delightful… always thought-provoking."

—Sheila Robertson

"This is a wonderful collection of poems gleaned from a long lifetime. Lothar's observations are keen and often funny, whether he's writing about politics, his childhood in Papua New Guinea, or events aboard a cruise ship with grandchildren."

—Cheryl Clark Lawson

"A balm for our times — this poet's bitingly honest, relatable & humorous poetry shares terse insights in a fresh format. A great storyteller of narrative verse, he leads us on a journey honed through years as a husband, father, citizen, seeker of truth, theologian: within darkness, the light still shines. In an irreverent take on life's foibles, we feel his reverence for the joy of our imperfect lives."

—Cheryl Richardson

For Carolyne

Poems Within This Volume

Whispers	1
A Knowing Silence	2
Holland America Cruise Line	3
Faces	4
Games of Dice and Cards	5
In The Dark of The Sun	7
He Loved Not Well	9
Kennewick	10
Mist	11
Ornamentation	12
The Weather Report	13
Songs and Lamentations of Prophetic Imagination	14
The Willows Wept in Perpetual Lamentation	16
Clam Mosaics	17
Time and Wonderment	18
Sand and Wind	19
Moonrise, Hernandez, NM	20
Six Stops, An Assignment	21
Roots and Ecstasies and Visions	24
Warmth	25
Rigidity of Line	26
Black and White	27
New Orleans	29
Hard Truths	30
In Postmortem Times	31
Five Day Book	32
The Hourglass	33
Present Tense	34
Digging In The Past	35
Remember Me	36
In The Beginning	38
At Lakeridge Lutheran Church Seattle, Washington	39
A Possible Creed	40

A Lenten Psalm	41
A Psalm of Silence	42
A Psalm of Thanksgiving	43
Psalm 23½	44
A Realist's Beatitudes	45
Holy Communion	46
The Sacraments	47
The Ending World	48
We Dare Call This Friday Good	49
Patterns in The Dust — A Psalm	51
The Mind's Connections	52
Angels Whisper	53
I Like A God	54
For Alexis On Her Birthday	55
For Anna	57
In A Pensive Mood On The Ship	58
Grief	59
Chorus from The West	60
Spring Cleaning	61
The Family Reunion	62
Portraits	65
A New Creation	66
Metaphor at Malalo	70
New Guinea Nightsong	71
Rain	72
Whether Apocryphal or True, I Leave It Up To You	73
Backyard Barbecue	75
History	76
History 2	77
History 3	78
History 4	79
Super Moon	80
Endnotes	
About The Author	

Preface

While I wrote poetry sporadically, say, in the fifties, I was encouraged when I got a good grade in college in a literature class (see *In the Beginning*, page 38). A year later I took a class on the poetry of T.S. Eliot. That interest in him and his work led to reading and studying his poems, plays, prose work and several biographies for the next six or seven years, writing papers, a thesis, an analysis of criticisms of *Murder in the Cathedral*, and so on (see the poem *We Dare Call This Friday Good* as an example of his influence, page 49).

It wasn't until 1996 when we still lived in the Seattle area that I entered a juried invitation to submit poems to the King County, Washington art program. I was accepted for *New Guinea Nightsong* (poem on page 71 and Endnote on page 85).

I joined the Live Poets Society in 2012 and have been an active member since then. Thus, after a very halting start over the decades, I now write regularly.

The format is arranged so that a date written in the lower right corner of the page indicates a completed poem. Lack of a date there indicates that the poem continues on the following page[s]. Poems with accompanying Endnotes will be so indicated with a subscripted number in the poem's title. Endnotes begin on page 83.

Finally, I am taking this moment to thank the members of the Live Poets Society for allowing me to participate with them. We share our poems at these meetings where the group suggests possible changes. Thus each poem is work-shopped. When I joined I made the decision to incorporate each of their suggestions into my poems. With two exceptions, I have followed that commitment and believe that my poems are the stronger and better for it. In listening and working with other poets and their work, I believe my own understanding of poetry and the poetic venture has brought me to a deep and abiding appreciation of poetry and profound enjoyment of the form. Nowhere else have I found a group of people who are both so gentle and yet so honest with each other. To members, past and present, I thank you.

I also thank Arne Pietz for giving me the impetus to put these poems in workable form. He has worked with the logistics and other technical aspects, the mundane work of setting up the whole project, and design, layout, and typesetting of the book. For that I am extremely grateful.

Whispers

The sun whispers to me in the morning;
I awaken to its golden sound
as gradually the ephemeral becomes concrete.

Consciousness rises like a diver surfacing,
or a soul lifting to heaven,
or an outfielder springing up to catch a fly ball.

There is resurrection when the sun whispers in my ear:
victory song of the sacrament of rebirth;
I rise anew.

If there is *petite mort* at night,
there surely must be *le grand reveil*
in the morning.

2017

A Knowing Silence

he sat there, going on and on
about very little
really nothing at all,
something not even worthy
of being called 'small talk'

air going in and out between
plush, easy, sometimes
deferential lips formed
syllables that in a different
context might have meant something,
here were just a substantial waste of time

oblivious, apparently, to his surroundings,
— or else nervous because the other two
weren't speaking at all —
maybe unable to stop,
he just kept rambling on

finally, exchanging a knowing silence
the other two arose
and, murmuring
Good night,
quietly left the salon
and stepped out into the chilly evening

January 27, 2018

Holland America Cruise Line

The company names its ships
after cities, dikes and dams in the Netherlands
Several years ago

we cruised on the *Westerdam*
this year the *Veendam*.
While in Amber Cove the *Rotterdam*

pulled up next to us. I recall
as a kid I read this wonderful
little book with two titles:

Hans Brinker or *The Silver Skates*
about this Dutch lad who lived
in a small city in the north of Holland.

I got real excited when I learned
they're naming a ship after Hans Brinker's
home town which in the novel was called Hot...

April 3, 2018

Faces

What does it feel like to live behind a face?

Those eyes
Droopy eyelid
Down-turned mouth.

Smile at the mirror.
You smile back — at last you see a friend.
Assess your face — is it kindly?
You hope so.

The guy who vacuums the carpet
Rearranges chess pieces on the board
As he passes by.

His face intensely interested in the rook,
The white rook;
Does he think of what it means to live
Behind his face?

The woman mixes together a Venti Mocha.
Does she think of her face beyond
Watching herself putting on make-up?

She smiles at a customer.
What is behind
Her smile?

July 11, 2019

Games of Dice and Cards

They sit around a table on the back deck.
He tosses the dice, a die falls to the deck.
The younger woman stoops to pick it up.

The older woman leans forward;
her long hair falls, covers one side of her face.
Their voices get louder — an argument?

He counts: *One, two, three, four....*
He reads from a card; puts it back on the pile.
I clearly hear him say, *I don't know how to die.*

He rolls the dice again. The older woman says,
Yes, you do. Now take another card.
The younger woman gives him a card from the pile.

He reads the card, stands, bows deeply to each in turn,
the older woman first, then the younger,
walks to the ship's rail, falls to a lower deck.

Neither woman speaks.
What is there to say?

July 13, 2019

In The Dark of The Sun[I]

There's a photograph of a man lighting a woman's cigarette
She leans over to cup her hand around his
As he holds the match; both are in front of
A large pool, a pillared tile-roofed building
Sits at the other end as a backdrop.

Dressed in tan double-breasted suit and dark tie
He stands on the pool's wide ledge
She wears a light jacket over a white dress
A clutch in her left hand a necklace visible
Both are slim.

They are standing between two very large urns
Luxurious plants in and around the urns
Completes the picture except for fading sunlight
Catching small insects and dust motes
In mid-air making the scene incandescent,
Neither insects nor motes move.

The photograph was taken in 1929;
There is a timelessness about it
That bespeaks a passionate intimacy, *a deux*,
Between the woman and the man.

As the moon darkened the sun to near-eclipse
Last week, the light in back of the home
Turned the stone patio and meandering stone path
An unearthly gray.

For once the moon did not reflect the sun's glory
Did not light up the ordinarily dark of the world
But hid the sun along a swath of the earth
During the time customarily set aside for the day.
Even the plants looked on in shocked silence
Sap draining from their stems and leaves
Till they looked pallid.
The stones lost their dark brown tones
And turned leaden in that strange
Gray blueish light.

Never totally dark the cool pale dimming sun
Might have touched the woman and the man
In the photograph, while they could have stood
Almost a century later not by a pool
But on those stones,
As the man lit the woman's cigarette.

September 22, 2017

He Loved Not Well

He loved not well,
Rather a certain guileless enthusiasm
led people to overlook
how badly he actually acted toward them.

When they found out, and disappointingly
left him, he was always puzzled, and hurt,
would point to his enthusiastic embraces
as if to say, *I did my best.*

But of course that is never enough,
as those of us who truly love can attest.
Love takes hard work
a pragmatic effort beyond ecstasy

beyond jangled nerve endings and
stimulated neurons
way past the paroxysms
of pounding hearts and grasping hands

toward that moment when the self is no longer
of consequence in the profound desire
to serve the beloved
to be willing to die for the beloved.

He never did learn that kind of love,
nor did his lovers ever find in him
the answers to their hearts' questions
that might have brought true joy.

March 18, 2018 (April 23, 2018)

Kennewick

This city is filled with people who harbor sad hopes:
The women, sitting in the restaurant,
Trying to look beautiful under
The 100-watt lights, without make-up;
The men wearing those ubiquitous caps
Like uniforms, men whose imaginations
Don't dare go beyond International
Harvester and Monday Night Football.

All this is gently oranged by little
Blinking jack-o'-lanterns, a Christmas idea
Translated into a Hallowe'en reality.
These women could have been beautiful;
The men could have been handsome, but
The moment of ecstasy turned them into
Shocked, harried, but superlative, parents.
And now they have no time for beauty.

If I loan you my body for a time,
Can you assure me, in turn,
That transcendence is possible?

Under the 100-watt light bulbs,
The answer must be, no.

Still, in the brown light of an evening's
Reminiscences, amid alcohol-thickened speech
And groping hands, they do discover
The incomprehensible and illimitable.
That moment passes; offspring remain forever.

October 27, 1997

Mist

I can live with mist,
White whisper beneath the moon,
And
Recall the dream beside the sea;
Still I cry to the sun for life.

Under the rain, I do not see blue wind;
Mystery reigns
Outside, near a city or village.

2000

Ornamentation

Dead windblown deciduous leaves
Cling to evergreens like
Yuletide ornaments.

2012

The Weather Report[2]

There is a chance of snow above McCall,
She said, as if to tell about
A wonderful event.
There's something to be said, I said,
About snow, I said, *above McCall;*
Sorta like the rain in Spain.
It's cold, of course, while rain is warm
Sorta like a girl I knew,
Cold in McCall, but warm in Spain.

2013

Songs and Lamentations of Prophetic Imagination 3

Sit by the River and remember the future.
Sing songs of joy and of freshness of youth.
Watch embers of long ago campfires
trail slight smoke into the wildness of the sky.

Ah, how spirits ride those gray threads
as they wander upward in the dark.
Stars do not move and clocks stand still
so moments of yearning can be discovered

and hours of time out of time
can build rapture upon ecstasy,
beyond breath and blood, yet in, with, and under
bodies of hope, pleasure and delight.

How do I do this?
He asked.
Do what, I said.
I don't know how to die.
Neither do I.

You've never died before; neither have I.
I do know some things about what happens when
a person dies, and I'll tell you as much as I know,
as much as you want to know.

This is the way the world works.
This is the way the world works:
the action is the seed,
potentiality is the culmination.

This thing has been known all along:
The weed of crime bears bitter fruit.
Martin Luther said, *We love the sin;*
it's the getting caught we hate.

Just before the car hits the wall,
the driver becomes sorrowful.
If, indeed, there were time, if there would be time,
the driver would weep at the future loss.

O, the wind-blown hair; the freedom of the road!
O, the sun-burnished arm; the heat of
the body snuggled up close!
O, the lips brushing a cheek in eager anticipation!

Listen to Earth sob as life is torn from her bosom.
See tank cars convulse and spit out black
greasy smoke into wildness of the sky
and push aside spirits trying to rise in the dark.

There is destruction at noon
and devastation in moonlight.
The faithless move mountains with bulldozers
more easily than those with faith.

Noise of calving glaciers
out-roars the storm's thunder
and the seas rise to carry
ice floes to warmer water.

The soul is separated from the body
for philosophical reasons;
the body is separated from
the world for purposes of exploitation.

Sit by the river and mourn the future,
even as the earth is destroyed
by those of brutish mien and greedy maws,
ravaging all beauty and adornment.

My world ends with my death. Mother Earth
dies more slowly, albeit with murderous intent
and wanton resolve by
those whose hubris knows no bounds.

March, 2014

The Willows Wept in Perpetual Lamentation [4]

That is one way of putting it;
though for humans, watching willows' limbs
drifting with a river's current,
lamenting in perpetuity might seem boring.

There should be some allowance, it would seem,
for revelry or exultation, some sort of balance
which suggests a natural ebb and swell
between one emotion and another.

But in current cultural and public life
contentment swiftly flows toward anxiety,
satisfaction quickly slips into anguish,
makes the idea of grieving feasible.

And not only feasible, but actually achievable
during daily perusal of most media outlets
as they report and comment on the latest
soul-jarring disruption of a former status quo.

At times like this the idea of perpetual lamentation
makes one want to join the willows.

June 20, 2018
June 29, 2018

Clam Mosaics

As I was walking on the beach yesterday afternoon,
I saw a number of pre-Pompeian, crushed clam-shell mosaics,
broken and tamped into the sand;
the joins perfectly matched and the patterns
quite amazing in their random characteristics:
as old as the first clam's shell broken on an ancient sea coast,
yet as new as this morning.

November, 1990

Time and Wonderment

A long time ago
when culture was young
the women took off their clothing
faced each other, smiled, and said,
Look!
Look, how beautiful we are!

And they became self-conscious.

The men faced each other
before time became important
removed their tunics and said,
Wow!
How magnificent we are!

and they became self-conscious.

They put their clothes back on,
their awareness enhanced,
exalting in the image,
they saw themselves
in all their wondrousness.

Ever since that time
we can see ourselves
— if we can see at all, —
ourselves in others.
Who we are in the eyes of those
who stand before us.

March 16, 2019

Sand and Wind[5]

Dune, White Sands National Monument
Ansel Adams gelatin silver tint, c. 1942

Caught with the speed of the shutter, the sand does not move,
and the weeds stand stock still;
Even the shadows know enough to anchor themselves
To the roots of the weeds.

So they are captured,
Now immutable,
Yet giving the impression of movement.

Suddenly sand ripples,
And plants wave.
There is wind, and no doubt,
Disturbing the sense of calm, playing tricks.

The sudden realization:
This sandbox belongs to the wind.

October 23, 2015

Moonrise, Hernandez, NM[6]

Ansel Adams, gelatin silver print, 1941

Time stood still that late afternoon
Just long enough to freeze a mystery
To hang a moon in the sky.

We have to tell what we see;
More important, we have to see what we see,
To penetrate the impenetrable.

Crosses mark the place where the dead reside,
The town behind them where the living abide,
And spreading across the landscape the *Sangre de Cristo* mountains
Hiding below streaks of wind-blown clouds.
Above all this horizontality the moon entire.

What we see in black and white is a mystic
Presence,
A sense that only the wideness of such a vista
Can encompass the incomprehensible.
Between earth and sky human habitation.

And quietly presiding over this vastness the moon
Between life and mystery the moon.
Between the mundane and iconic the moon.
O, the moon!

August 20, 2015

Six Stops, An Assignment

STOP ONE

The air — so liquid —
it flows above below around.
I don't count the breathing in and out,
but that's part of it's sweetness
like a child's breath.

How gently it touches my face,
like a lover's stroke.
It seems to disappear into another world
but teasingly lifts the paper I've written on
and drops it again just out of reach.

In the meantime it has let loose of
the smoke, dust, particles of detritus
deposited these in other places.
Thus cleansed,
I see through to the next mountain.

STOP TWO

Without that dust and dirt
a perfume floats around and about anyway
maybe not a perfume but a hint of something
ephemeral drifting around in the sunlight.

I can't quite grasp the delicacy
my nose is too crude to catch
— much less name — the beauty
of the air in this place.

STOP THREE

Insects use this air like highways
moving from here to there
carrying cargoes of food and drink for their use.

Others wander around on invisible byways and trails;
still others strike off on their own
making their own paths to who-knows where.

STOP FOUR

My sister moved when she was twelve
returned to her birthplace when fifty.
The minute she got off the plane she said,
I smell home!
Oh, how wonderful!

Her husband said,
That's just the jungle and the sea.
But she vehemently insisted,
That's what my home smells like.
And she stomped her foot for emphasis.

STOP FIVE

They say there's no sound in a vacuum
but here I can hear the grasshoppers clatter away
when I get in close.

Further into the woods
I can hear birds yelling at each other
as they move along on the air's freeways.
There's even a stream sloshing around nearby;
maybe I can smell the water, maybe.

STOP SIX

Air involves all the senses:
too dusty or smoky you can't see
air carries sound like nothing else
feel the wind and you know it is good
smell its humor as it tickles your nose
even air can taste good.

All the while the image of the wind lures me on
to try to discover my own paths through its wilderness.

August 19, 2018
(8-19-18 a Palindrome)

Roots and Ecstasies and Visions[8]

She lived on roots and ecstasies and visions,
Not on texts or pears or pomegranates.
Desert terrors bring chimera,
A sense of running in absence of air,
Where it is difficult to inhale.
It helps to stand outside the self —
If the self is real.

Vision commingles self and
Other; without both there is nothing.
Without root there can be no ecstasy;
Without both there is nothing.

The joy of release
Is not running from self
But running along-side self and
Other;
Because she cannot know for sure,
Because she cannot know,
She finds ecstasy and vision in root.

The more she runs
The lighter her feet
Till eidolons keep pace
And space means absence of air
In trackless terrors of the desert.

November 16, 2018

Warmth

I slide onto the mattress.
She's already asleep,
Virtuously, though quietly snoring.
Fully half of the bed clothes are —
Like a mantle of grace —
Wrapping her in solemn splendor,
Or providing shy, demure, and modest cover.

My side of the bed, meantime,
Has been swept clean of sheet, coverlet, the works.
But I, I rest in the warmth
Of the knowledge that I have crossed three
Of the first five most splendid bridges in the world:
The Sydney Harbour,
The San Francisco Bay,
The Florentine Ponte Vecchio.

August 19, 2016

Rigidity of Line[9]

Fluidity of bodies in motion
Combine and recombine
Attempt yet again to flee gravity.

All take shape
Fructify one another
In wonder, awe, and mystery.

How can such stasis bespeak motion?
How can that which is bounded
Seem without substance
Yet consequential?

November, 2015

Black and White[10]

Black dress cut perilously low in front

Black hair pulled tight in back

Black dress slit — in the center —
above the knee, mid-thigh,
dangerously high

Black thoughts turn to white heat,
imagination walks faster than the

Black hair, or the long, black dress.

March 18, 2016

New Orleans II

There's a place in New Orleans called
Preservation Hall where old retired guys go to play jazz.

There's a building called the Mint which
used to print monies for the USA and the CSA.

There's a little book shop where
William Faulkner lived for a short time.

There's a wonderful lady in New Orleans
called Lauree

There's a cathedral which has been
upgraded to a basilica.

There are architectural styles in New Orleans,
reflecting French, Spanish, and other influences.

There's a professional football team
down there dubbed the Saints.

And there's a Cool Cat in New Orleans
named Lothar.

December 15, 2017

Hard Truths

I always thought of myself as a
Gentleman Farmer
Until I met this woman who
Told me I certainly
Was no gentleman.

Then all my peas died
Even though I'd watered
And fertilized them as well,
So I came to the conclusion
That I'm not much of a farmer either.

July, 2014

In Postmortem Times

They did a *premortem* on a man who was not dead
Called it gall-bladder removal, they did
Maybe an appendectomy
Something sinister I'm sure.

They used the word *exploratory* often
In their post-op talk, they did.
Careful to get him out of the hospital before
He died so as to keep their records unbloodied.

Some thought it odd they didn't use
Anesthetic of any kind
But others knew they secretly gave him whiskey,
So much it almost did him in.

One surgeon got mad they didn't save any
Whiskey for her.
Aah, but they had a secret stash and she
Got over her anger mighty quick, she did.

Once out of the hospital, the man did die,
So they hurriedly changed
The technical term to *postmortem*
And it's been that way ever since.

May 18, 2017

Five Day Book

DAY ONE

I think I will comfort the comfortable
and disturb the afflicted. Maybe that will
help people see how necessary the violin
is to Western culture. If it doesn't, I'll
have to try some other method.

DAY TWO

For some reason there has got to be a
beginning and an end. We don't seem to be
able simply to exist.

DAY THREE

The rain reaches the earth eventually,
plopping down in little globules of clear
liquid, with all the arrogance of a human being.

DAY FOUR

The comedian, Sid Caesar, once told this joke:
I've got a brain that's gone out of its mind.

DAY FIVE

Every day I learn a little more about
the future; I've already learned over sixty years
of future. Just ask me.

1986

The Hourglass

I have an hourglass at home,
but it's flawed; it only runs for five minutes and
then you have to turn it upside down
and repeat eleven more times.
I keep losing count.

I also have trouble boiling a three-minute egg.
That's so arbitrary anyway; I just let it go for
the full five minutes, what the heck.
Doesn't seem to hurt the eggs.
The neighbors don't mind either.

I went to the plant store
and bought some German thyme
but it died right away,
so I wasn't able to save any.

I had this girlfriend.
People said she had an hourglass figure.
I got worn out turning her upside down
every five minutes.
She didn't like it either.

When they say *time ticks away,*
you know they don't have
an hourglass: sand doesn't make a sound.
I keep getting worried there's a lump in it
and it will get stuck at three and a half or four minutes.

When they say, *Time's running out,*
you know they have an hourglass,
otherwise they would say, *Time ticks away.*
But nobody knows where "away" is, or
where it's running to.

People will try to fool you into telling you,
It's in the past.
But none of them know where that is;
just ask them.

May 15, 2018

Present Tense

Inexorably
Jack-booted days march by
Followed by guns of months
And tanks of years,
While decades fly over in tight formation.

Worriedly
We binocular the skies wondering
If our force is large enough
To stave off timelessness
Ever-present enemy of time.

Strangely
We seem to desire the immutable
When it is really time itself
That we hope will not end
Or cease to be.

October 6, 2016

Digging In The Past

I'm very much interested in digging up
bones of past experience, reconstructing
flesh and hair with clay words and old, cast-off metaphors,
to help you see what I once looked like.

Here's a bone deformed from infancy
for example, results of emotional
psychological power wrongly given
wrongly accepted wrongly utilized.

Here's one bent by powerful expressions;
closer looks reveal hollow intellect,
superficial understanding
and caches of trivial information.

We see bones now long-buried
give us ample evidence when brought back to life by
breathing hard into post-Adamic nostrils.

May 12, 2018

Remember Me

I want to be remembered
forever
never forgotten

but maybe
more importantly
who might that remember-er be.

If you
loathe me now
please forget.

If you hate the sight of me
go out and get
Alzheimer's.

Would
love it
if you adore me

will approve if you like
my intellect
or intuition.

Remember these
but
above all
my good looks.

A Greek Chorus

A certain poignancy
may be seen by those who
agree with this sentiment

latent lugubriousness
in the all too obvious
attempt at comic relief

a clear thirst for iconic
immortality
a quest in uncertain times.

Being good may last for a day
a lifetime's excellence
is another matter.

So it is with those
who would wish
for eternal greatness:

fleeting, fickle, unfaithful
lasting no longer than idle thought
on a summer's day.

September 30, 2018
October 9, 2018

In The Beginning[12]

Ἐν ἀρχῇ ἦν ὁ Λόγος
The Word
Can we think,
Is a man?

καὶ Θεὸς ἦν ὁ Λόγος
The Word
Can we think,
Is a god?

ὁ Πατήρ μου παντου μείζου ἐστιν
God, God,
Can we think of you at all?

Tamoc Taŋ gômwa undambê...
The smoke
Of my incense
Rises to Thee.

1957

At Lakeridge Lutheran Church Seattle, Washington[13]

With Bill now dead, we move on by.
With Wilhelmena also gone,
We pause to thank our God
For each of them.

We say some sainted words, —
Archaic now, in one score years, —
Still fraught with sacred sound;
We pay respect, yet know not how.

October, 1992

A Possible Creed

I believe that God is an act of will
a creative movement
an originative moment.

I believe that Spirit is a dynamic force
animating inspiring engagement
removing impediments to action.

I believe that Jesus is a lively function
engendering human response
to creative movement
and the call to action.

I believe that the Church
lives out its life
in love, decision, obedience
to will
to force
to function
in absolute loyalty
not in absolute principles.

December 3, 2018

A Lenten Psalm

The Lord patiently waits for his will to be accomplished;
>the Spirit broods on the nest of chaos.

My soul desires all things now,
>and the future to come at once.

The Lord's day may be as a thousand years;
>I want my thousand years packed into a single day,

each moment crammed with a year's delight,
>each twinkling of an eye filled with months of joy.

God endlessly tinkers with his evolution;
>the waiter dallies too long with my pie.

Shorten the forty years of my wilderness
>into forty days of Lent.

Lengthen my fifty years of ministry,
>but shorten my three-day grave.

Hold off my death,
>but hasten my resurrection.

1990

A Psalm of Silence

I know that God is just in all the world
        and glorious is his name in triumph.

But nothing happens, my voice is silent;
        my mind is a dry summer day.

Isaiah could sit there in his desert,
        waiting for a swampy heaven.

Meanwhile he filled several meters' length
        of palimpsest with inspired poetry.

If only I could rhyme two or three lines;
        if only I could pen a quatrain!

If only I could be inspired for a moment;
        I have begged God to help me speak.

But he has not given me speech;
        inspiration is an aorist verb.

My paper just rests quietly;
        my pen sits beside it, stiffly.

Still, God needs no testimony from me;
        he is great and glorious even in my silence.

My simple boast, thus, is in God still;
        I do love God's goodness and justice.

He who is almighty above all else,
        loves me even in my silence.

1991

A Psalm of Thanksgiving

Each plant has its own environment
    wherein it worships God.

Each tree soars, or bows, in thanks;
    each bush loves its creator in its zone.

Animals, too, know their place,
    and are content to cry their approval to God.

The lion on the veld munches zebra
    and gives thanks to God for food.

The miracle of the feeding of the
five thousand buffalo on the plain is repeated daily;
    daily they celebrate with thanksgiving.

But humans have no perfect habitat;
    Eden is no more, therefore everywhere
    must be.

So, human thanks takes many forms,
    and comes from many places.

What a grand chorus this makes!
    What harmonies are thus created!

1990

Psalm 23½

As I gaze with my mind's eye, I see into my spirit;
with my inner sight, I learn to know myself.

I stare at me, staring back; sometimes I get a blank look,
sometimes I resist insight out of fear, or myopia.

Self-delusion's eyelid is heavy;
I cling to my story with tenacity.

My self is a labyrinth;
there is a Minotaur lurking in its center.

The twists, turns of my life's passageways
have been created by myriads of sensations,

each adding its own cul-de-sac;
I fear not the boulevard, its the alley I dread.

Go into the dark, my spirit tells me;
stalk the black pavements.

It's just fine for the Psalmist to say he fears no evil;
he hasn't glimpsed the monster in the middle of me.

I've seen its tail a time or two, maybe its shoulder once;
I've heard its bellow and have smelled its spoor.

My enemies are eating my lunch; I can't find my cup anywhere;
I've no depth perception, for my mind has only one eye.

Let me look inward again;
give me a stout string, long; and a tallow.

Anchor the string at the entrance;
I shall try again.

1990

A Realist's Beatitudes

Blessed are they who worship the Bible,
>   for theirs is an unchanging view.

Blessed are the pious,
>   for they shall be self-satisfied.

Blessed are they who are always right,
>   for they shall be able to say, *I told you so.*

Blessed are they who never break the law,
>   for they shall be self-righteous.

Blessed are they who never curse nor swear,
>   for theirs shall be a world without righteous anger.

Blessed are they who refuse to learn anything new
>   for they shall always be wise in their own conceit.

Blessed are they who always did what their ancestors did,
>   for they shall never have to be confronted with anything new.

Blessed are they who are "self-made,"
>   for they shall never need to be charitable.

Blessed are they who are perfect,
>   for they shall never have to know forgiveness.

All Saints Sunday
November, 1983

Holy Communion[14]

What often starts out as a feast of unity,
Finishes up as a food fight in a cafeteria.
Taboo in Eden was a single piece of fruit
From some mysterious tree.

However, here there's wine or grape juice,
Unleavened wafer or gluten-free, or
A torn piece from a large loaf of wheat,
Till unity looks like a smörgåsbord.

I'll have a snifter of Mogan David.
Shot glasses are so gauche;
Then a slice of Russian Rye. I'll dip the rye.
Thank you.

The communal element seems lost
In the haste of walk-through lines,
Lacking momentary pause
To find or even seek concord among fellow guests;

Reminder of old English pub calls for last rounds:
Hurry up, please, it's time,
Hurry up, please, it's time,
As if the sanctuary is about to close.

October 27, 2018

The Sacraments[15]

To the font we've all been brought;
won the battle, which he fought;
not because of our great love,
but in his merit.

Through the sea, and through our death,
Christ restores to us our breath,
that we may see the heavenly dove,
and kin inherit.

For death in these cold waters
makes us all sons and daughters,
and declares this from above:
Christ's words to us: share it.

Welcome to the sacred nave;
blood and bread he freely gave;
this we share with you thereof:
Christ's cross: we wear it.

April 26, 1997

The Ending World [16]

As I sat dying in my chair,
sitting by the big picture windows,
the blood vessels broke in my eyes,
I suppose from pressure in my blood,
and my vision was covered with crimson.
I called out: *'The skies are blood red;*
the end of the world is at hand;
the Messiah is coming.'

And then the drums of my ears were broken,
I suppose from the whealing blood,
and there were screeches in my ears.
I called out: *'The trumpets of God are sounding;*
this puny world is closing;
the Messiah is here.'

We found his body like that, the next day,
sitting by the big picture windows,
unseeing eyes staring at the blood-red skies,
watching angels swooping among the clouds.
Ecstasy, terror, shaped his lips, his cheeks;
alizarin tears formed crusted tracks,
while spittle dried on his chin.

Great drops of blood had burst from his ears,
cascaded down and onto his
shoulders. Unseeing eyes told us
he had heard God's trumpets blowing
the victory songs of the sacrament of rebirth.

His vision thus came to fruition, slumped in the chair
by the big picture windows, while my companion,
moving her wings carefully out of the way,
gently lifted him up and flew out to where
he could worship God amid the rest of the angels
archangels, and all the company of heaven; and he
humbly took his place among the redeemed.

September 12, 1996

We Dare Call This Friday Good [17]

To tell the truth, I'm selfish.
Yet, I dare call this Friday good,
since it contains for me the salvation
I cannot achieve by myself,
but long for and yearn after, nevertheless.

It wasn't that I didn't try
to earn my own salvation.
I turned the other cheek;
I held the hands of the sick;
I stood in the dock with criminals,
and I mourned with those whose parents had died.

I filled sandbags on a levee for four days.
I drove through snow no one else would.
My phone rang at midnight and I answered
the need on the other end.

Finally, the burden was too great.
I never knew when enough was enough.
I never knew if I could take a break,
or go on vacation to get away from it all.
What if God wanted just one more thing from me?

Well, that's what happened.
Jesus wanted me near him in his hour of need.
But all I could give him was
a sense of foreboding
that this Friday might not end the way
he had hoped it would.

Not only did I abandon him,
at the last even God seemed
to run in the other direction.
Crucifixion was too personal for me,
and God is a God of love after all.

The only one who seemed to stick by him
to the end, was the Evil One,
waiting to escort him
to the realm of the dead.

The light of the world grows dim this day;
it must not be snuffed forever; it can't be so.
The last beat of that great heart
echoes in my ears.

I feel my own heart throb in dread and dismay,
because I fear that pretense is all there is.
In the end, the Evil One has to be cheated
out of another soul.
The Evil One cannot win, must not win.

My body is carrying on
this frightful discourse:
my heart, my head, my knees,
my neck, my hands
howl out their apprehension.

And I long for the uncertainty of
my own good deeds,
even as I see clearly how they have failed me.

So, I must trust that God did, indeed,
snatch Jesus from the Evil One,
and I must learn to rely on those who saw.

This can be the only way
I dare call this Friday good.

1994

Patterns in The Dust — A Psalm[18]

We begin: the moon rises
                only to set again.

The sun comes and goes;
                the pattern is fixed.

The Koheleth has said this before;
                this sermon grows out of the same text'
That which is old is new;
                that which is new must be old again.

Earth's dust is our womb;
                the sun sets the pattern.
Round and round
                we are born and born.

We grow, we thrive;
                this sermon derives from the same text:
Remember, you are dust and to
                dust you shall — yes, by all means, — *return*.

In the meantime, O, yes;
                in this sole meantime,
this dust kicks its heels!
                this dust rides the earth's wings!

2014

The Mind's Connections

Someone said, *Better write that down;*
we'll forget it soon enough.

But Miriam said, *Don't ever use my name.*
I'd feel too self-conscious.

So, there we stood, not saying anything.

Remembering.

Do lions remember? Do they enjoy gazelle as much
as we enjoy fall's first apple?

Is memory real, or is it a cerebral construct to keep
us busy, while we digest
last night's cheese sandwich?

On what winds does the Spirit send me to find
what spiritual place in memory for our need?

1986

Angels Whisper [19]

Angels whisper in my ear
And I tell just what they say,

We'll be seeing you
And when we do
We hope you will consent to travel, too.

Will there be endless hills
Green and warm,
Or dry and parched land
Horned toads scudding along arid deserts,
Or swampy savannas
Pathless waterways of floating islands?

What was Eden like
Where I'm following you
Will it be like that,
Or will it be a rest in peace
Sleep from now on
Gone when mem'ry fades?

I sit alone in the room at night
And yearn to know the future now
See it stretch out in twist and tangle
To learn, find, endure, sustain
Is that too much to ask?
Should I ask again?

I truly desire nothing less
but sit here
"A man in a Hathaway shirt"
Dressed not quite ready
To go anywhere
The angels lead.

September 28, 2016

I Like A God

I like a God who can be surprised
Whose days are filled with joy at life
Who can be pleased with gifts of love.

I like a God who loves a practical joke
Who can laugh when taken in
Who prattles with children.

I like a God who enjoys the scenery
Who genuinely likes people
Who likes to play board games.

I like a God who likes to create things
Who has a sense of humor
Who understands nuance.

I like a God who appreciates irony
Who can handle ribald humor
Above all, I like a God who likes me.

August 20, 2017

For Alexis On Her Birthday

There was a time
indeed
there was a time
when you were small
and, as with all small children,
your mind was open
to larger things.

Eager to learn to walk
to learn to speak
to play as if it were work
to show others what you have done
to find joy
to discover hurt
all these you learned then.

Now this time
indeed
this time
now that you are taller
wise to the world
your mind is able to grasp
ever larger things.

Your future is opening
wide and wider
as you comprehend
the vastness of choice
the possibility of intellectual pursuit
the thrill of adventure
the dreams of future experience.

There are times
indeed
there are times
when the future is frightening
and you may wish
to be small again
to be comfortable again.

But be of good courage
and learn to endure
learn to overcome
learn to prosper
live life with a flourish
so that they say of you
you are uniquely wonderful.

October 15, 2019

For Anna[20]

Courage is the ability to fall into an abyss,
not jump, but actually fall,
like the game played at team-building retreats
where you stand on a chair and fall backward,
knowing, no, hoping others at the retreat
will catch you.

Courage is the startled
realization that you are in the midst of doing
somethings others will later call heroic
all the while, astonished, you ask
Who pushed me?

Courage is concluding
that failure to act is in and of itself
an act of cowardice,
and for some unknown reason,
you do not wish to be called a coward.

Give me your great glaring vices, and great glaring virtues,
but preserve me from neat little neutral ambiguities.
Be anything you like, but for pity's sake,
be it to the top of your bent. Live fully,
live passionately, live disastrously.

But above all else,
be courageous.

December 21, 2018

In A Pensive Mood On The Ship

For Kaitlin

There is a quiet but persistent sound
gently permeating the silence.

My granddaughter sleeps behind me.
I use the make-up mirror light
not to disturb her as I write these lines.

As the day closes its eyes for the night,
peace enters through the stateroom door.

I am content.

2019

Grief

There are different forms of grief:
loss of one's parent, spouse, child,
or even pet, house, country.

These griefs are all past tense:
loss of my sister, parents,
places I've lived, people I've known.

Then there are events in my past,
great moments, hours, years
which I did not wish to end.

This is where we can insert loss of
opportunity, grief over missed chances,
failures, wrong action.

Let me pause for a moment to weep
in the past tense, for that which is no more.

Now I'm finding, at my age,
something new and different,
which is why I use the term *past tense*.

I now have discovered future grief,
anticipatory grief, heartbreak
over that which has yet to occur.

It is not death itself, I think:
rather, a sadness of what happens in
the future when I will not be around.
This fills me with anguish,
near despair, sorrow, an awful sense
of not knowing the future — forever.

And I pause to weep for that which is not-yet
to grieve in future tense.

January, 2019

Chorus from The West[21]

We stand here almost at the Western edge
Of this land, waiting and waiting for the
End, the final opportunity to
Bid adieu, to say good-bye, or even
Good night. .... Since God is immortal, does he
Know what it means to die? There are some doubts.

That's brutal; for him not to know, but to
Bless-curse us by giving us awareness,
Forcing us to out-do him, to be better.
Of all the power, authority, we
Now take away omniscience. For we
Know mortality, but this God doesn't.

Still, we ask God to bless this ground, this soil,
And his presence now to give us comfort. ....
Honor, O God, those who also know more
Than this God will ever know or endure.

November 21, 2010

Spring Cleaning

Spring cleaning in the
Winter of life brings to mind
My grandmother beating
The rugs with a wire beater.
It took her and my mother to roll
Up the rugs and carry them out
To the wire line.

All my mother heard was the
Thud of my father's shoe on the floor.
That, in essence, was the last
Word he ever spoke.
Entering the room, she saw him
Sitting there, staring.
My mother and my wife stood there.

There's a newly sanded, finished kitchen floor.
Next comes a new carpet.

May 17, 2017

The Family Reunion

DAY ONE

In the Name of the Father,
And of the Son,
And of the Holy Ghost;
he who eats the fastest gets the most.
AMEN!

My sister gave me a book about Norwegians
I discovered I'm a Viking.

We drove up to these famous dunes,
And there was a sign that said,
No parking in the sand.
So I stopped there. But then I saw
Another sign that said,
Daytime parking only.
So I pulled up there
And got stuck in the sand.

I've traced my family tree all the way back,
And so far I'm back to 20 AD

He was offered 165,000, but turned it down.
A YEAR!!!

I'm never gonna drive this far again
In my whole life.

Here I am eighty, and I discovered I'm a Viking;
Good genes I can tell you.

They started giving this stuff to race horses,
And farmers learned that they could use
It on cows, too. Some guy decided to
Squirt it on his shoulder, and now I use it all
The time. Can't get it in a drug store;
You have to go to the horse section of
The farm store. Sometimes it burns,
But it is really great stuff. It loosens
Up your muscles or something.

We drove clear up from Mississippi
To our cabin in northern Minnesota;
Now we're down here.

They're flying in later this morning
And flying out this early evening.

Well, that's better than last time.
Last time they only stayed two hours
Before going back. At least now
They're going to have to stay
Until the plane leaves again.

DAY TWO

Rub-a-dub-dub, thanks for the grub;
Yay, God!
AMEN!

He was going to be a millionaire,
But then he lost the farm.

They got this extremely right-wing religious
Education — they had a shotgun wedding, you know —
And they had a bunch of kids.

He's gradually losing track of reality.

I want to move to Upper Sandusky
But he won't do it.
I can't hardly get up stairs anymore;
I want a house on one floor, but he won't budge.

We've got to fix up the place
To get it ready for sale.

You're going to sell the house?

Yeah, we want to move away from Minneapolis
To Stillwater, to a townhouse there.

What needs fixing?

Well, for one thing the previous owners
Just cut a few holes in the heating ducts
In the basement; we have to fix those.
The previous owners
Sure didn't finish the house at all.

You've lived there
For a long time
As I recall.

Yeah, forty years.

What did he die from?

He ate high fat foods in the kitchen
And walked to the chair in the living room
And sat and watched television.
I was so mad, I nearly took that television
And smashed it on the floor!

But what did he die from?

Well, I just told you: he ate fat foods
And watched television.

I know, but what caused his death?

I dunno.

God be with you till we meet again;
By good counsels guide, uphold you,
With a shepherd's care enfold you.
God be with you till we meet again.

O God our help in ages past,
We don't know future tense.
We think the present is all right,
But tomorrow makes no sense.

O God, our help in ages past,
We wonder if you live;
If it is so, would you, at once,
A sign to us please give.

2005

Portraits

They're all gone now:
Aladu, Eremiah, Katam, Filemon, Ludi,
Yasasau, Lois.
To miss them means to ache for some moment
In time,
Some hope that this must not,
Cannot end in my memory only.

Look at Lois: she's still twenty three,
Still wearing the same dark dress.
The randomly placed alphabet letters (A. B. C.)
Are there on her white collar. She always
Looks straight ahead with a slight smile.
Am I still nine?

Aladu stands there in his white, long-sleeved shirt,
Dark tie, white *laplap*, heavy black belt, barefoot.
He's twenty five. I must be twelve.

I must bring time past to the present;
There must be, there has to be another
Chance to learn the song Eremiah
Tried to teach me.

Yearning is not enough. I must touch them, *Tok Pisin*
Once more, love them so they can acknowledge it.
It's either that or they're living a life that
I've not yet lived.

Are they longing to see me,
to *Tok Pisin* to me?
Do I live in their memories only
As they live in mine?

2014

A New Creation

I

The crack of dawn, they say,
And don't know what that means,
Except that the spinning of the earth
Gives us the feel of a gradually opening door,

Where the light moves into the room,
Or leers from behind the mountains daily,
Only to die in the sea later, to drown
Quickly, and without even a cry for help.

Still, it is very good to watch,
Though I did not, unless I was ordered to.
Parents can be merciless about such things
As getting up at the crack of a very first dawn.

I shall always be grateful to have been born in the late
Afternoon, the time before dark, the time when the sun,
Seeing its work almost accomplished, decides to
Allow the night its due.

II

*The only difference between
The rainy season and the dry season is that it rains
More in the rainy season,*
My father used to say. And we'd all laugh.

But, my, it always was a good rain. And the creek ran clear.
I could see all the way to the stony bottom,
Crayfish down there looking for dinner,
Or trying to hide from us.
We went to movies shown in a corrugated tin roofed building;
It rained so hard on the roof we couldn't hear the sound track.
That was okay, 'cause people smoked so much we
Could hardly see the screen.

That too was okay, since we were very interested
In girls, and this was a moment in the dark,
In the noise of the rain,
And cool damp of the night.

III

They say the Taimi islanders have star maps
So accurate they can sail their double prow
Canoes out of sight of land for days at a time;
It took me nine months just to spot the Southern Cross.

By that time I didn't care.
All I knew was that those stars and moon
Were the best ever sources
For a youngster to use to dream heroic dreams.

IV

One feature of the tropics is how fast vegetation grows.
I built a *liklik haus,* a small shack,
Out of limbs from a nearby tree, roofing it
Over with corrugated tin.

Four weeks later
The shack was
More like a tree house,
Leaves growing out all over.

But how marvelous it all is! How
The bush grows.
The struggle, as noisy as sunrise,
Grasps life with greedy hands.

V

Watch the wallabies abound (pardon the pun);
While cassowaries, taking note
Of a lull in the activities,
Wander around chatting among friends.

Whatever creeps, runs, stalks,
Or leaps is likely to be found someplace here,
Except anything larger than a wild pig.
And that's just fine with me.

Whatever happened in time past,
Wallabies decided not to remain kangaroos,
But stubbornly went off in their own direction.
Cassowaries snubbed their beaks at emus.

But the beauty and style that came from these
Resisters is most exciting to behold.
The results are breathtakingly
Beautiful.

VI

Aladu was stout, square-built, people said,
Wonderfully strong.
Strong enough, indeed, to let me wrestle him
To the ground once in a while.
I see him now as wise, both teacher, friend to me,
Wood carver, father to his children,
Faithful husband to his wife,
A man of great integrity.

Yasasau was tall,
Good-looking, yes, even tempting,
Though she would have denied that;
Given to singing songs.

Sharp of mind, witty, with a strong
Sense of self, yet not overbearing
Not pushy, as they say;
A new woman though she didn't know it.

VII

As I look out over the railing on the back porch
Of my mind, all these images fan out across
The landscape and I sip green coconut juice as I relax,
Provided thus with a great view of what it was like,

Of what it will be like
Sometime again,
An endless visit longer than memory lasts.
And I rest. And, indeed, I rest.

2014

Metaphor at Malalo [23]

Invited to a great festival at Malalo,
We left Lae to cross the Huon Gulf.
The Maneba, sixty foot copra ship, carried us
In grand style.

Having just read 'Treasure Island,'
The sea beckoned as never before,
And I saw me standing at the helm,
Chasing pirates.

At twelve, even a copra ship was exotic.

I asked my parents, they said,
Ask the skipper.
He said,
Ask the man at the wheel.

I asked the great question of the man-at-the-wheel,
And then we talked for a while.
Encouraged, I dared ask again,
And he pointed out
That he'd already stepped back.

If you use your imagination, you could see
A smudge on the horizon:
Let's call it Malalo.

But I saw no compass, no sea map.
The man-at-the-wheel said,
Keep the wake straight,
and we'll get to Malalo without delay.

2016

New Guinea Nightsong[24]

They sat around the fires at night
And tuned their drums with wads of sap
The snake skin heads sang in return
And told us all that all was well.

Each night a mother's heart I heard
In beating drums and fell asleep at peace
And do so still as I recall those drums
Though half a century has passed.

1996

Rain

Here I am, an old man, sitting in an oriel,
Straining to hear rain pat a taro leaf,
Pummel a corrugated tin roof,
Five thousand miles and fifty years ago.

I sniff the dusty air around me, and
Desperately try to smell the tropic rain
Once again before I forget forever
What it has meant to me.

That rain was solace and comfort for me.
The memory of it cheers me still,
Even as its echo dies away.

2014

Whether Apocryphal or True, I Leave It Up To You 25

Fifteen New Guineans with
Machetes and sarips cleared
The bush to carve out an airstrip.

The heat of the day (from noon to three),
And the damp of the air (from the sea),
Made them long for rest.

But the European had no sympathy;
Kept pushing them to finish the project.
He needed cargo the planes would bring.

A young lad, running up from the station,
Came to the European with an urgent
Message for him to return immediately.

The fifteen exchanged smiles of relief;
Rest was within their grasp.
Eagerly they looked for places to sit.

Short lived: the European had a glass eye,
Which he plucked from his face
And set it on a stump.

That eye would watch and tell him who was who
And what was what and who had worked
and who had not.

The New Guineans resumed work,
Each vying to look good for the eye,
Each worried what the eye would see.

Until one man
Grabbed a large taro leaf,
Crept into the bush,

Circled around from behind
And ever-so gently
Lidded the eye with the leaf.

And the fifteen New Guineans smiled
and rested from the heat of the day
And the damp of the air.

2014

Backyard Barbecue

Sitting in the back yard
under two large umbrellas
on the patio, the place where
living happens,
there to entertain
acquaintances, relatives.
The hostess asks politely,
And what are you doing lately?

The answer drags on for
half an hour or more
until the host asks,
*What do you plan to do
in the near future?*

The answer to that
slogs along for another
mini-eternity and then
the guests stand and
blithely announce that
it is time to go home
to feed the dog.

The hostess and host
wearily pick up the
empty glasses and dishes.
*A little gossip could have broken
the tedium*, he says.
She replies, *Maybe they
think it's impolite to ask
how we are?*

And so they settle down
in the family room
to watch a little TV
while the dishwasher
cleans up the evidence.

September 9, 2020

History[26]

History is permanent
the future is temporary
till it's the past.

In spite of the language
time is not a never ending river;
a timeline is convenient fiction.

History is perception of
chunks of experience that keep
rising to the surface of our minds.

We insist on tying these chunks
together until they appear
to follow one another.

Rather, clumped
they simmer
on the back burner
of our minds
until
we taste them once more.

But simmering changes history
gives it richer
fuller flavor.
It's never Déjà vu
all over again
but hints of something different.

They say
stew tastes better the next day
the mix has a chance to swap flavors.
For some, history
tastes better after years
simmering on the back burner.

July 21, 2020

History 2

History is not one damn thing after another,
rather a bunch of snapshots all jumbled up
resting quietly in a box, or piled in a heap
at the bottom of a dresser drawer
to be removed from the box or drawer
and looked at on a rainy Sunday afternoon.
Flip through the photographs very quickly and,
like the film in a projector, projected on a wall,
they seem to move in sequence.

In this picture here, I'm three, no. . . , four.
This shot is at Eagle Point Park
in Clinton, Iowa

Here's another one; I'd say I'm still four.
We used to go there practically every Saturday
and Pauline always brought
her new Brownie Box camera along.
By summer's end she'd almost worn it out.

The phrases — *every Saturday, always brought,*
and — *by summer's end* are all fiction.
Only the photographs tell the truth.

August 1, 2020

History 3

Action completed in time past;
that's the definition of an aorist verb.
I went to town.

Time, they say,
*is nature's way of making sure
everything doesn't happen at once.*

This sentence: *I will have been going to town*
is merely a convention we agree on
so everything doesn't happen all at once.

But everything happens at once
and we're just having fun
playing around with the language.

If each occasion is discreet, alone,
we invent continuity
to keep from going mad

just like we expand our end-of-the-world experience
of death to cosmic end-of-the-world projections
in order to feed our hubris.

If I am to die
why, then, it's only fitting
the whole universe should go with me.

For all practical purposes, for me,
whatever happens to the universe
it must do it without me.

Still, everything does happen at once
and we're just having fun
playing around with the language.

August 2, 2020

History 4

The past is a foreign country,
they do things differently there.
—L.P. Hartley

Back in the ol' town after years
Main Street looks un-Mainly
businesses closed, new ones in place
old buildings gone, empty lots overgrown

Couldn't find Home Street
now renamed Strange Avenue

the house is addition'ed
swing set nowhere in sight
Somebody tore out saplings
from the front yard
transplanted mature Maple, Linden, Elm
leaves heaped high raked by the wind

Odd name plate by the front door
even the sun casts unusual shadows
cracks all over the front walk
young neighbor (?) looks askance

They don't even speak the same language

sounds similar but disconnected
I'm but a stranger here.
New Town's my home.

August 20, 2020

Super Moon

O the moon shines tonight on pretty Redwing,
the breezes sighing, the night birds crying.
O the moon shines tonight an pretty Redwing
but she is crying her heart away.
Dad used to sing this song when I was a child
Maybe after dinner when we were sitting around the table
Or in the car at night.

These are the only lyrics I recall now.
But tonight the moon shines on me
As I stand at the rail of the cruise ship
The sea reflects the road
The great moon lays down for my feet.

Similes strain and crack, still cannot
Really express the whiter than white light
This super moon lavishes on the darkness.

The idea of the moon floating around out there
Long after I'm gone and forgotten stings my ego.
Petty of me to think the moon should wane before I do.

The moon's increases make it easy, though,
To hope my life could also be renewed.
Still at my age I have to be grateful that the moon
Should let me see its glory this one chance more.

2015

Notes On Selected Poems

1   *In The Dark Of The Sun* was inspired by the eclipse in 2017, which was ninety-some percent total in Boise, Idaho; I made a connection with that event and a photograph in *The New York Times Book Review* of Michael J. Arden and his wife taken in Cannes in 1929. The event and photograph in some sense haunts me still and will be linked in my mind always.

2   *The Weather Report.* Driving one day I heard the radio announcer read the weather report. I pulled off to the side of the road to copy down what she said, because I immediately recognized she spoke in iambic pentameter. Her sentence became the first line of the poem.

3   *Songs and Lamentations of Prophetic Imagination* is from *The Prophetic Imagination* and *The Practice of Prophetic Imagination*, titles of books both written by Walter Brueggemann. Lines 13–20 are from "Dying Well," a handout at an adult class at King of Glory Lutheran Church (Boise, Idaho) on February 12, 2014, led by Dr. Anne Palma. Line 26 is from the opening of the radio program "The Shadow." Lines 27–28 are from What Luther Says (2:1028), Ewald Plass, ed. Lines 43–44 are from First Corinthians 13:2.

4   *The Willows Wept In Perpetual Lamentation* is from a line in Virginia Woolf's *A Room of One's Own* (1929).

5   *Sand And Wind* was written after viewing a photograph by Ansel Adams. His title of the photograph is just below the title of the poem.

6   *Moonrise, Hernandez, NM* is also named after an Ansel Adams photograph title.

7   *Six Stops, An Assignment* was written at a Writing Workshop retreat held at Luther Heights Bible Camp in Stanley, Idaho, led by Susan Rowe. The assignment was to stop at six specified locations in the woods and write something at each spot; here presented are the results of my efforts.

8   *Roots And Ecstasies And Visions* is from a line in Dostoyevsky's *Crime and Punishment*.

9 *Rigidity Of Line* was written for the program "Folding/Unfolding," using Origami imagery through contemporary dance and poetry. The program was performed in collaboration with The Off-Center Dance Group and the Live Poets Society in Boise, Idaho on January 13, 2016.

10 *Black and White* was written while I was in a Starbuck's coffee shop in Shoreline Washington, idly looking at pedestrians walking to and fro outside.

11 *New Orleans.* While on a Road Scholar tour in New Orleans, Louisiana, our guide told me that she volunteered for a local veterinarian, helping to get kittens ready for adoption. She said she liked to give special names to these animals and, because I had such an interesting name, she asked if I would give permission to lend my name to the next kitten. I was honored, but would give permission on condition that she send me a picture of the lucky little guy.

12 *In The Beginning.* The first and fifth lines are from John 1:1 in Koine Greek: "In the beginning was the Word" / "And the Word was God." The ninth line, also in Greek, is: "My Father is greater than all," a reference to God. The twelfth line is the first sentence of the Lord's Prayer ("Our Father in heaven...") in Yabim, one of the languages spoken in Papua New Guinea. The poem was an assignment in a college literature class.

13 *At Lakeridge Lutheran Church, Seattle, Washington* contains two lines (lines two and three in the second stanza) which are references to *The Lutheran Book of Worship.* The members of this congregation were not used to using the ritual for funerals in the book; thus, for them was "archaic," though only "one score years" old.

14 *Holy Communion.* "Hurry up, please, it's time" is from T.S. Eliot's "Ash Wednesday II A Game of Chess."

15 *The Sacraments* was written in response to a request from the Coar family, Bainbridge Island, Washington.

16 *The Ending World* is a collaboration with Leslie D. Foster, who wrote the title and the first two stanzas.

17 *We Dare Call This Friday Good* is a line from Four Quartets, by T.S. Eliot.

18   *Patterns In The Dust.* The term *Koheleth* is Hebrew for 'teacher' (can also mean 'preacher'); the author of Ecclesiastes is traditionally identified with King Solomon. The last two lines in stanza four hint of Ecclesiastes 3:20, but come directly from the Ash Wednesday Liturgy.

19   *Angels Whisper.* The reference to the Hathaway Shirt comes from a 1950's advertisement by a popular men's apparel company.

20   *For Anna.* The quotation is by Vita de Sackville West.

21   *Chorus From The West* was written in memory of Effie Ione Christopherson Link.

22   *Portraits.* The word *laplap* is Pisin for loin cloth. The phrase, "tok pisin" means "to speak in pisin — a kind of pidgin or dialect language" which suggests a certain intimacy based on the fact that we both speak the same language.

23   *Metaphor At Malalo* was first published in the annual Writers In The Attic anthology, titled *Water* (2016), sponsored by The Cabin, a non-profit literary organization located in Boise, Idaho.

24   *New Guinea Nightsong* was first published by the King County (Washington state) Public Arts Program, "Poetry on the Buses," in coöperation with the King County METRO System. The general theme for the project was "Telling Our Stories."

25   *Whether Apocryphal or True....* The word *sarip* is Pisin for a tool used for cutting grass and weeds. The poem is based on a story circulated in Papua New Guinea long before I heard it in the 1950's. Everyone I've spoken to acknowledges having heard it, too. But no one seems to know the identity of the European, making me think it is some kind of urban legend, or, in this case, jungle legend. Still, what really appeals to me is how the New Guinean used his own worldview to outsmart the European.

26   *The History Poems (Inclusive)* were inspired by an online article in which the author suggested that time is simply individual discreet events which have really no connection with one another. Intrigued by this idea, I ended up writing what turned out to be actually a kind of series about what the concept could mean.

About The Author

Lothar was born on Ragetta (now known as Kranket), a small island off of the coast of Madang, Papua New Guinea in 1936 to Lutheran missionary parents. He graduated from Pacific Lutheran University in 1959 with a B.A. in Literature. He then went on and graduated from Wartburg Theological Seminary with a Masters in Divinity and then ordained into the Lutheran ministry in 1963. He received an M.A. in English from Northern Michigan University in 1969.

He and Carolyne Link were married in 1960. They have three children, ten grandchildren, and five great-grandchildren. They are now retired and live in Garden City, Idaho.

Lothar has served parishes in Illinois and Idaho; as Campus Pastor (and adjunct faculty) in Michigan (also sponsored by The United Presbyterian Church, U.S.A.) and Nebraska; and as an Interim pastor in fifteen congregations in Washington and Idaho (the last four in Episcopal parishes in Idaho) all of which spanned five decades of dedicated and fulfilling service in the ministry.

CPSIA information can be obtained
at www.ICGtesting.com
Printed in the USA
FSHW011610040221
78234FS